Polar Bears

Focus: Endangered Animals

Meredith Costain

Polar bears live near the North Pole.

Polar bears live on the ice and snow.

Polar bears swim in very cold water.

Polar bears hunt for fish in the water.

Polar bears have thick, white fur.

Once people hunted polar bears for their fur.

Now people protect them.